Power Climb

Growing your small business

James McBrearty

Published 2012

© 2012 by James McBrearty.

ISBN 9781849143035

BNI® the VCP Process® and Givers Gain® are registered trademarks of BNI.

taxhelp.uk.com® is a registered trademark, 2582169.

Front cover image © Paul Hampton - Fotolia.com

Index

3

4

Introduction

In aviation there are several limiting factors affecting how high and how fast an aeroplane can go - positive factors of thrust and lift, and negative ones of weight and drag.

In business it's a similar situation with both positive and negative factors affecting how high and how fast a business can grow. In the business world some of the many factors can be knowledge and time, finance available and the market.

In both situations, there are things that can be done to improve performance and make things easier - it is always a balancing act with differing factors affecting each other.

Whilst we all have the same amount of time each day available to us, what we do with that time makes a big difference - working harder has it's physical limits, so working smarter instead is the only way forward.

A favourite quote of mine, by Gail Nott, is 'you've got to learn more to earn more' and this is very much what I've found myself over the last six years - starting a business from scratch and growing it year on year in some difficult economic conditions.

In many cases now when growing a business, money doesn't have to be a limiting factor - thanks to the resources available it is possible to have a huge impact without much outlay, investing time instead - provided you know where to look for advice and support to maximise your impact.

Market conditions are always changing, in the past you could get by doing the same things that had been done before, but this is no longer the case (as many industries have already found out, and others will do.) Now, you have to keep developing a business constantly just to stay in the same place.

The old saying 'if you keep doing what you've always done you'll get the results you always have' no longer applies in business.

In this book I share some of the tips I've found over the last six years, dealing with small self-employed businesses (and starting one myself) I have come into contact with hundreds of business owners and many of their issues are the same.

My first book Chocks Away, published in 2010, covered how to combine online and offline networking to grow a business and these are still skills that can assist business growth today. However, things are constantly developing and particularly in regards to social media two years is a long time. Some of my advice has therefore been updated in this regard.

Starting, running and growing your own business is one of the most rewarding things you can do - and my aim in sharing my experiences is to assist you in your own business, so you can earn more money *and also get a greater return on the time you are investing.*

Acknowledgements

I would like to thank the following people, who have continued to help me on my journey and who I personally recommend. I owe much of what I know to them and the knowledge that they have freely shared:

Ivan Misner

Dr Misner is the founder of BNI, the world's number one business referral organisation. Through BNI I have been able to develop my presentation skills.

From initially speaking to only a few people at my local BNI meeting I am now comfortable presenting to groups of over a hundred, and have also presented internationally.

www.bni.com

Fiona Humberstone

Fiona owns the Flourish studio in Guildford, they are brand stylists and have helped me since the early days of my business.

From starting simply with flyers, we progressed to the taxhelp.uk.com logo and stationery - leading to a complete redesign of the website in early 2012. I have received excellent feedback from clients regarding the website, and it works in the business generating referrals for me 24/7.

In addition to this, Fiona runs courses at her studio to assist business owners - I have attended several, including her branding master class which I highly recommend. The points I bring up in the branding chapter came from Fiona.

www.flourishstudios.co.uk

How to use this book

I would highly recommend you read the branding chapter first as this could save you wasted time and money later.

After that, please do pick the topics that are of interest to you personally from the index, and read them in the order of your own preference.

The old days of the business book, where you have to start at the beginning and work through it - reading through pages of topics that are of no personal interest, are thankfully passing.

If you are reading this on kindle it's even easier, thanks to the index and search functions available.

At the end of each chapter there is a 'questions to consider' page - please do take the time to think about these & write down your answers:

Knowledge is only useful if it is applied, and your written answers can form the basis of your action plan.

Branding

You may think it's a bit 'back to front' starting the book with a section on branding, indeed you could be thinking that branding is only for large companies and doesn't apply to you at this stage.

Except, you may find that you could save yourself a lot of time and money later by taking a moment now to consider branding.

I've heard of people that have spent thousands of pounds on new websites/stationery/etc, thinking that they will deal with the brand at a later date - unfortunately in some cases when they do, it could mean that the best option is then starting again from scratch, wasting all the time and money they had invested to date.

Fiona Humberstone made some excellent points online in 2012:

Do you need a decent brand to succeed?

I'm not suggesting for one moment that your business will fail if you don't have a decent brand, but you're certainly making life more difficult for yourself.

If you know exactly what your business is all about, who your ideal clients are and what they value about what you do then you can communicate with them in a way that puts your business to the top of their list.

If you consistently communicate with these customers and prospects in a way that inspires and resonates with them then they'll ache to work with you: whether you're the cheapest or not.

And if you can show confidence and professionalism throughout all of your communications: website, printed collateral and through all the social media channels then when these ideal clients and prospective customers find you, then why wouldn't you blow your competitors out of the water?

Once you've got all of this right, spending money on advertising, search engine optimisation and pay per click marketing makes sense. Why? Because you need people to find your business!

But you need people to see your business in the way you see it, and too often there's a discrepancy between the confidence and passion you have for your business and what people see on the outside.

Start with your brand and build up your marketing from there but make sure you get focused. Because business without focus is incredibly tough.

Questions to consider

what do you offer - specifically?

who are your clients and where are they located?

What makes your clients choose you instead of a competitor?

how you want them to feel?

Sales & marketing

Who works in sales & marketing? *You do.*

If you are like many business owners, you started your business to do the things you love. Sales and marketing probably weren't high on the list yet now these are additional tasks that you need to include.

This could involve a marketing budget and learning more about marketing, tasks you may not have budgeted for in either time or money.

With Social Media it is possible to generate interest and new clients with just time as an investment - indeed several people I know have built their own website into one of the top ranked sites by this method.

You can usually exchange time for money when it comes to marketing, but you should be aware that your own time isn't free as it is potentially costing you billable hours. You should also consider the differing quality of results from doing things yourself as opposed to hiring a professional.

If you believe some of the negative stories in the press about the economy and don't invest in marketing, you could find that this actually results in those stories becoming true.

A great story to illustrate this, is the famous one about the hot dog seller:

"A Man lived by the side of the road…and sold hot dogs.

He was hard of hearing, so he had no radio.

He had trouble with his eyes, so he had no newspaper. But he sold good hot dogs.

He put up a sign on the highway, telling how good they were.

He stood by the side of the road and cried, "Buy a hot dog, mister!"

And People bought. He increased his meat and bun order, and he bought a bigger stove to take care of his trade.

He got his son home from college to help him.

But then something happened. His son said, "Father, haven't you been listening to the radio? There's a big Depression on.

The international situation is terrible, and the domestic situation is even worse."

Whereupon the father thought, "Well, my son has gone to college. He listens to the radio and reads the newspaper, so he ought to know."

So, the father cut down on the bun order, took down his advertising sign, and no longer bothered to stand on the highway to sell hot dogs.

His hot dog sales fell almost overnight.

"You were right, son", the father said to the boy. "We are certainly in the middle of a Great Depression.""

Marketing is a continuous process, whether it is paid for by time or money.

However, with the current financial situation, now is an ideal opportunity to get ahead as your marketing will be more effective when others are cutting back as there is less noise to distract people.

It's something I did myself in 2012, offering a discount for tax returns early in the tax year. Whilst it can be somewhat unusual for discounts to be offered by an accountancy practice, there is a win win for both myself and the client.

The client saves money on their accounts and tax return, as well as having the reassurance that their affairs are completed ahead of the deadlines.

Once they know the tax liability for the year they can then plan for it and concentrate on their business rather than worry about tax. The benefit for me is that it reduces the year end workload, and increases capacity to take on more new clients in January 2013.

I have noticed a few other companies use marketing strategies for a win/win – for example my garage recently ran a promotion for a free health-check on your car, together with a free breakfast and also including a complimentary car wash and vacuum.

From the customer's point of view the benefits are obvious, for the garage it continues customer contact, as well as potentially allowing preventative maintenance to be undertaken should it be required.

What exactly do you do?

When it comes to new business there's a common mistake people can fall into – not being specific in what they are looking for.

People may think that their potential client base is wide and while it may be, if people aren't able to focus on an area to look out for then they are likely to miss potential opportunities to refer you. Potential clients may also think that you do not deal with them either.

A good way to remember this is 'if you ask for anyone and say you can do anything, what you will actually end up with is no one and nothing!'

It's something I've experienced myself – specialising in helping self-employed people in Surrey – so people instantly know who we help and where we give a face to face service. Interestingly, I do get people asking for other services that I don't offer – but with an extensive network of connections I can usually recommend someone suitable to help them.

I also had a great example of how powerful being specific is, when I attended a European networking conference in Glasgow. Several of the presenters asked for specific referrals at the end of their presentations. Despite being 400 miles away from home, I was able to connect three of them to people I know.

Had they just said what they do in general terms, and not been very specific, then they wouldn't have achieved the results.

When you are thinking about bringing in more business, you could find that narrowing your focus and being specific actually brings in **more** business, not less as some people fear.

Regular client contact

Keeping in touch with clients is important, particularly now in the current economic climate when competitors may be cutting back. You may choose to do this perhaps by regular mailings or newsletters, there are always opportunities to keep in touch.

There are always seasonal events that give you the chance to stay in touch, such as summer competitions/etc.

An example of this from my own business is Christmas cards. It may be another area where people are thinking about cutting back, however there are good business reasons for sending these:

1)   Maintaining client contact is very important.

2)   There are other alternatives such as electronic cards, however in a digital world there is still a place for real paper cards and they do stand out.

3)   For ourselves, December and January are the two busiest months of the year. We specially arrange our workload so that we are able to take on new clients at this time of year, when other accountants may be turning people away, so being visible is important.

When you consider the benefits, the cost of the cards and postage is very affordable and justified. We commissioned our own card last year, and it was a very easy process.

One of the options would have been to include my signature printed on the hundreds of cards we sent out, however I chose to sign each one by hand as I think it is important.

In recent years I have seen companies send an e-card with a note that they are going to make a donation to charity instead. Rather than choose this route, I sent paper cards and also made a charitable donation.

Our Christmas card is somewhat unusual when compared to the normal cards people receive...I choose the image of a business jet in the snow as it has several relevant meanings, ranging from the fact that we help clients businesses take off to the fact that I have been a qualified private pilot since 2000.

No cost/low cost local marketing

There are also usually opportunities to increase your visibility, at little or no cost, in the local community.

For example taxhelp.uk.com are supporters of the Elmbridge Borough Council's more discount card. The card allows a range of discounts to holders, from local businesses to leisure facilities – by offering a discount our business is promoted for free in the local community.

Perhaps there are similar schemes in your area? If not, you could always approach the local chamber of commerce or consider starting something yourself between local businesses and sharing the cost.

I have seen local business groups combine their resources and produce a leaflet advertising say 15 businesses on it. This means that the individuals costs are much lower, and there are always opportunities for developing referral relationships with the other members as well.

Questions to consider

Do you think a win/win promotion could work for you and your clients?

What exactly do you do, who are your clients and where are they located?

What low cost/no cost marketing opportunities are available to you?

Websites

Online, your website is a public face, a salesperson working 24/7, and one that people are increasingly using to judge your business.

As such, it is worthwhile investing money into its appearance and ease of use.

Before we look at content issues, the first thing to consider is the actual domain name. Whilst some people may advocate a long name full of keywords, you have to consider the possible loss of business from potential clients who either can't remember your address or who can't be bothered to type it in.

Perhaps they may even go to the bother of trying to type it in, only to find that they made a mistake but can't be bothered to find it - instead going to a competitor. If your email address follows your domain name format, then the problem could be compounded.

You may think one way around this is by using a Quick Response (QR) code. These are the square graphic symbols that have been appearing on advertising and some business cards.

They have their place and can work, depending on their application, however you have to consider how 'quick' they actually are.

The user must take out their phone, load the QR reader app and finally hold their phone so it captures the QR code using the camera.

Sometimes it's easier to just use a short web and email address that will make it simpler for people to reach you.

I had been researching local businesses at the start of 2012, which has exposed me to over 1,500 different websites.

Unfortunately, I found that many of them are continuing to make the same mistakes – ones which are costing them business and making it easier for their competitors, despite being straightforward to fix.

Here are a few:

The site has gone – if people find you through a directory or search and then go to your website only to find an empty error page they are likely to assume that you have gone out of business. Perhaps you have a new website, but it may be worth keeping the old one as a redirect to the new site. If people go to your physical address and it's empty they assume you have gone out of business. At least with a building sometimes people put a note in the window telling people where they have moved to, it should be the same online.

Contact details – the purpose of many websites is to generate enquiries for the business. If this is the goal, then it should be made easy for people to contact you, and to know who you are. If you just have a business name with no personal details you are less likely to receive enquiries – people do business with people. You also want to make it easy for people to reach you, by whatever method they prefer, whether that is by email or telephone or via a social network.

Location – I have noticed some sites not actually telling you where they are located. For a limited company it is a legal requirement that the registered address is shown on the website, as well as the other contact details, yet some sites don't tell you anywhere where they are located. Some other sites have started posting vague statements about areas they cover – that might bring them search results, but when local people are looking to do business with a local company they are going to be less than impressed that they are based maybe 100 miles away but 'cover' the area.

Email address – there are three aspects to consider. The first is whether it is made easy for people to contact the company – complicated forms with large numbers of compulsory boxes will drive clients away. The second is the actual email address. It is very affordable to have a personal email, rather than a free account. When people are contacting the business, if they see that they only have a free email address it will affect their impression of the business. The final aspect is to ensure that the email address is a valid one – if people receive a bounced email error after taking the time to write you a message, it is as bad as a sales person that just walks away after the potential client has taken the time to explain their issue.

These are several of the points to consider, which are all simple and low cost options to increase the business generated from a website. Depending on how the website content management system is structured, they should be able to be changed in minutes rather than hours.

Website evolution
Websites should evolve over time, and it is good to regularly review yours to make sure it is up to date.

Many sites have a 'current news' section or a blog. It's important to remember that if you have these sections, you will need to plan to ensure that you are going to regularly update them. A top news item from last year, or a blog with only a couple of postings in the last few years are actually going to count against you in people's impressions.

What would you think if you were in the waiting room for a business and the newspaper or wall calendar was a year old?

You can also look back in time at your own and competitors websites using something called the Wayback Machine – a site that archives web sites.

Looking up taxhelp.uk.com I found that their archive goes back to 2007, which is useful in chronicling the site since then.

Using my own site as an example, I can show the evolution of one site and how things need to develop constantly in order to stay up to date:

2007 – I was using a site that I had written myself. Whilst providing all the relevant information a potential client would need, this lacked the professional polish that a web developer would bring.

2008 - Saw the commissioning of the new website, at considerable cost. Whilst this looked good, I could no longer update the site myself – something that's important with the constant changes occurring in tax. However, an introduction back in 2008 by the web developers actually turned out to be the company I used in 2012 for the latest update.

2009 – This saw a return to my own ability to update the site, having purchased professional web design software myself and learnt how to use it. It also saw the introduction of video on the site, with several videos I had shot to further explain the service being used.

2010 – With the emergence of social media this saw more options on the site for sharing, as well as links to several of my online profiles.

2011 – Blogging has been something I've done since 2009, so it made sense to integrate this to the taxhelp.uk.com website – so that I can provide tips that can be useful to clients, as well as keeping them up to date. It also saw the introduction of the trademark.

2012 – The site was completely redesigned, giving a much improved site for the next stage of the business development.

Looking back to 2007, it's amazing how far my own site has evolved from the early days

When you are working on your website content, it's important to remember that online claims are now covered by the Advertising Standards Authority.

The ASA's online remit now extends to cover companies' own marketing claims on their own websites and in other non-paid for space they control. This brings enhanced consumer protection, and we have already seen companies taken to task for unreasonable claims in their marketing.

Security online

Finally in this chapter, we come to the issue of online security and hacking.

Business websites continue to be attacked, costing owners both in time spent trying to fix them as well as in lost income.

In a speech in 2012, reported by the BBC, the intelligence agency's chief has said that MI5 is battling astonishing levels of cyber-attacks on UK industry. Jonathan Evans warned internet vulnerabilities were being exploited by criminals.

Small business owners may think that this only applies to large companies – however it very much also applies to them as well, even if they just have a very simple site.

Depending on who manages your website will determine how threats are protected against. If you have a website manager then they will deal with this for you, however in many cases this may be the business owner themselves.

Below are some simple security tips you may want to consider for your own site – with websites and search engines being a primary source of new business, ensuring their operation is important.

Updating the website software. If you have a site run on a platform such as Wordpress then there are regular security updates included with new versions. It's important to install these when they become available, as they usually close loopholes in security that were being exploited.

Passwords. The password used to access the website, both the backend hosting account and the content management system, needs to be robust. It will probably not need to be entered often, and can be stored on a secure computer for access anyway, so can be very long. Using this long password (perhaps 40 characters or more) with a mixture of upper and lowercase as well as non alpha-numerical characters will increase the security.

Backups. If you are using Wordpress or similar then you can easily export a backup file of your posts and updates. However this does not back up all of the site, so a more comprehensive backup solution would be beneficial, perhaps in addition to the normal site backup. Utilities such as FileZilla will enable you download a copy of the entire site, including all the backend files. This makes it easy to upload and restore the site in case of any problems or hacks at a later date.

Testing & Monitoring. Whilst looking at the site yourself on a browser will give you information on whether it is working well, it won't tell you about another type of hack – the search redirect hack. This is where the site is hacked so that when people find it on a search engine, they are redirected to another site via hidden code on your site.

One way to check for potential issues such as this is to try searching for pages on your site using search engines, click on the link and make sure it works. The other is to install monitoring software that gives you reports whenever any file on your website changes. This enables you to confirm that the file change is expected rather than being done by someone else.

You can also install analytic software to your site and monitor the level of hits coming from search engines – a sudden drop could signify problems with the site.

In addition, there are also services that will monitor your site and report if it is unavailable by email, so that you can then check on the situation.

The great benefit of these security points above is that they can be straightforward to set up, and will ensure that your website remains working and generating referrals for you 24/7.

Questions to consider

Is your web & email address easy to use?

How has your website changed since it started?

Is the current news on your site still current?

What are your security and backup procedures for your website?

Entrepreneurship

You may have heard of Michael Gerber's three roles theory for business owners…

As a business owner you now have three roles you need to manage instead of just the one you thought you were going to do:

- The technician. This is actually performing the work you set up your business to do.

- The manager. You need to step back and plan your workload to ensure that deadlines are met and workloads managed, perhaps by engaging assistance.

- The entrepreneur. You must also plan the future direction of the business, whether that is new markets, methods or products. This ensures that the business continues to grow.

Entrepreneurship is increasingly important, staying the same actually means you are falling behind in today's fast changing business world.

I regularly attend courses and take time out from my business to engage the entrepreneur and investigate future opportunities, as well as undertake training in new areas.

It's an important part of my success, and something that could be worthwhile to you as well.

One day out of the office while writing this book was to attend a branding master class follow-up meeting, where I discussed advanced branding opportunities with fellow graduates from a range of local businesses. Having this time out increased my productivity when I returned to the office, as well as reinforcing the choices I had made so far.

If you think you can't afford to take time away from the business you should remember Gail Nott's words:

"You've got to learn more to earn more"

Risk taking?

Some people consider that entrepreneurs are risk takers, in my own research I found an interesting study asking 'why do pilots make better CEO's?'

I'm a pilot myself, holding both European and American licences since 2000, so it had particular relevance to me as I'm also a CEO as well.

The study raises some interesting points, yes you do have to take risks when starting and growing a business – however these should always be calculated ones rather than just sensation seeking!

When I am flying an aircraft I'm always looking at ways to minimise the risks. One of the ways to do this is to study reports of incidents that have happened to other pilots and what they did to ensure a successful outcome.

It is also something that can be done by the self-employed – too many times business owners make the same mistakes, when studying the methods behind the successes of others could make all the difference...

When we are looking at risk taking, if you know someone who is still employed and considering self-employment then there are opportunities.

By being flexible, and if their employment contract allows it, they could even start that self-employed business **today** and operate it on flexible hours outside of the 9-5.

This can be a good way to start a new business – they still have a regular income from employment and can also work on their self-employed business around that.

Initially it may just bring in some useful extra income, but they are also building up the foundations of a successful business that could support them should anything happen to their employed role.

And it also makes things easy when they decide to switch to being full-time self-employed. It is much better to have a business with several months operation and experience behind them than to start one up suddenly from scratch. It takes time to get things set up and develop relationships, and they can get ahead of their competitors.

There is also an additional benefit, that many people don't know about, of tax losses. When you start a business there are normally quite a few expenses, even if you are minimising the costs. It could be that they have a loss for their first year of operation after taking account of these. If they do, then they can actually get tax relief for this by claiming it against the employed income they have had in the year.

This could bring in a well needed tax refund, that could be reinvested in the growth of the business.

Business funding

I have talked about how in many cases time can be exchanged for money in order to grow a business. This is particularly relevant with the restricted access to funding many people are experiencing, leaving them with limited options.

There are interesting financing alternatives developing though, indeed some initiatives that were sent to other countries are actually coming back to be used here.

Particularly in the current climate, now is an ideal time to invest in the future and for growth whilst your competitors are downsizing and restricting their marketing efforts.

There are usually limits as to how much an entrepreneur can invest in their own business, so when that point is reached something that may be of interest is crowd funding.

Crowd funding is simply the process of bringing together private investors to invest amounts in growing businesses. Similar to the Dragons TV show, but with normal investors rather than multi-millionaires.

There can also be the incentives of bonuses for investors as well. By spreading the investment through many investors it makes it easy for people to choose which pitches to support.

Downtime?

I'd like to discuss, in the middle of this chapter on entrepreneurship, downtime.

You may think that you are looking to grow a business, not take time off, so what does this have to do with me?

What's the most important asset in your business, and on which the business relies?

It's you.

Many people that run their own business find that, because they love their business, they end up spending a lot of time on it.

For those of us who are inspired by our business, this doesn't seem like 'work' such as a 9 to 5 but it is still important to make sure that you are also having sufficient down time in order to stay at peak performance.

Whether this is by ensuring regular holidays are scheduled, or making time in the diary for your hobbies, it is important not to let this slip.

Quite a few accountants have a nightmare time in January with the personal tax deadline – indeed I usually work seven days a week in January myself and also have many late nights working.

In January 2012 I was seeing a client out in the country at 9pm one night for example. However because of this, I knew that I could take time off one Sunday morning in order to indulge one of my own hobbies which is general aviation.

I normally fly single-engine airplanes, however unfortunately these are not allowed over central London, but twin-engine planes are and I happen to know someone who has one…

We flew from London Biggin Hill airport, which is a short flight to central London. It was an ideal day for flying and we flew over many of London's landmarks.

Afterwards, I returned to the office refreshed ready for the remaining few weeks coming up to the January deadline.

It's important that you take time out of the business to ensure your own performance, in whichever way you find that helps you relax and 'switch off' for a time.

Working ON the business

Taking time out from the business to plan for the business is also an important task as an entrepreneur.

A good time to do this, in addition to normal regular reviews, is at the end of the year - indeed it is something Dr Ivan Misner does every year:

It's hard to hit a target you're not aiming at. The new year is a great time to think about some of your plans and goals for the next 12 months (and beyond). Even if all you have is a couple days, take the time at the end of every year to slow down and do some "vision making" for your business. Remember that a successful businessperson needs to work "on" the business as well as "in" the business

Sometimes a day out of the office may be what's needed, in December 2011 I attended a focus workshop that enabled me to take a whole day planning for the future. Yes, there is a cost both in terms of course fees and billable time - but when you return to the business you will have a greater focus and will be more productive.

Other benefits of networking

Running a business used to be lonely, but now with all the opportunities for networking online and offline it doesn't have to be.

Every business needs someone you can bounce ideas off and benefit from their experience. Most situations you will encounter in business will have already been experienced by someone else, so rather than waste time trying to work things out yourself why not benefit from the knowledge of people who have already done this?

When I launched taxhelp.uk.com back in 2006 I didn't have this support for the first couple of years and found things quite difficult. I also made a few mistakes that I wouldn't have done if I had been able to benefit from others experience.

In 2008 I started networking online and also joined BNI, this gave me regular access to others in business and I was able to bounce ideas weekly and also benefit from their own experiences.

For many people, this can be a powerful way to help develop your business in addition to the actual new business generated directly through referrals.

Big business?

When people are only seeing reports talking about big business in the press, they may think that small business doesn't matter.

I'd like to share a couple of facts I learned from Frank DeRaffele at a BNI directors conference in Manchester:

Did you know, From 1980-2005, firms less than 5 years old accounted for ALL net job growth in the USA. Europe is similar.

Did you know that in the US-99.3%, in Europe-99.1% and in the UK-98.9% of all employer businesses are small businesses?

So when people are talking about 'big' business it's important to put things in perspective in regards to the contribution that small business actually plays.

Industry changes

Finally in this chapter, I revisit some of the points from the hot dog seller story. When you're reading news articles it's important to realise that perhaps the author could have their own opinions clouded by their impressions, which could lead to inadvertent sabotage.

One of the claimed sources of how the word sabotage came into use is from the Netherlands in the 15th century when workers would throw their sabots (wooden shoes) into the wooden gears of the textile looms to break the cogs, feeling the automated machines would render the human workers obsolete.

I've heard the changes occurring in business now likened to the industrial revolution, which I think is an ideal way for people to think of these.

The music industry has already been through massive changes with the introduction of digital delivery.

The print industry is currently in the process of change, with Kindles/etc. starting to replace paper for the delivery of content. There are already more books sold by Amazon on kindle than in print now.

The TV industry is another one where changes are coming. In the past you needed an expensive TV studio and/or equipment, combined with many staff to produce content.

Now, my iPhone can produce broadcast quality HD video, which can be edited on the phone and then uploaded to YouTube – then shared with millions of people and at very low cost.

Indeed, many people 'time shift' their TV watching so that it fits in with their own needs, rather than the times the TV stations prescribe that you will watch something. It's also affecting advertising – if people are watching a prime time programme in the morning was it worth paying top money for the evening prime-time advertising slot when they didn't watch it then?

As people 'time shift' their programming many fast forward through the adverts anyway. This is one of the reasons product placement is increasing in use, and with digital delivery of programmes there are no adverts anyway.

These changes are something to be mindful of when reading or watching reports from the traditional media on the rise of the new economy.

Changes in business are something that I have experienced myself in my own industry, for example how I became 'the twittering tax man' and as a result presented to 85 chartered accountants about Social Networking, something I wouldn't have thought to be doing a few years ago.

Questions to consider

Do you have time away from your business planned, so you can work on it instead of just in it?

Who do you know that has always wanted to start their own self-employed business but hasn't got round to it, because they think it's a risk?

What do you do to relax, and are you making sure it's blocked out in your own diary?

What are your plans for the business? This year? Next year? In 5 years?

Can you foresee changes in your own industry, that you can start making plans for now?

Your 'office'

In the past it was a straightforward plan, you started a business so you had an office. You commuted to it, and your clients came to see you there.

When you step back and consider the situation you realise that there are better options, that reduce costs and save time for both the business owner and their clients.

It's been reported, in a survey by Direct Line, that commuters in Manchester are spending nearly two hours every day commuting. Whilst this is supposed to be the worst in the UK, many people are spending considerable time commuting every week.

One of the advantages of self employment is that you can generally avoid commuting – many people do not need premises and can work from home. There is also the flexibility of choosing your work hours.

Suddenly you may find that you have an extra day per week that you can use, compared to people commuting every day.

Being self-employed also gives you the flexibility to operate outside of the 9 to 5, both in times and locations.

Indeed it is something I've adopted myself – I can visit clients in the early morning, evening and at the weekend, meaning that the 'rush hours' are avoided.

Because you don't need a physical office, it is also worth considering how to stay in touch when you are either with clients or in meetings.

You may think that it's ok if you have voicemail on your phone - except quite a high percentage of people won't leave messages for you, particularly if they are new client enquiries.

There's an easy solution though, by using a virtual assistant. There are many of them now offering their services, and you can divert your phone calls there and they will take a message for you whilst you are unavailable.

You may find that many of your clients also operate from mobile offices themselves, using their mobile phones to make calls rather than a landline.

Whilst mobile phone contracts include a monthly allowance for calls, unfortunately many of these contracts do not allow calls to 08 numbers as part of the package – so these become chargeable calls.

We have operated an 0845 number on the main line for some time, to ensure that clients calling us were only charged a local rate call – however with the growth in numbers of people running their businesses from a mobile we introduced an 03 number as well.

03 numbers are charged as a normal call from a mobile and are included within the free inclusive minutes of the contract, so this is something that you may want to investigate yourself.

You can register online for an 03 number and have it connected to your mobile phone, so you don't even need to have a landline attached now. The benefit is you now have one fixed number that can be connected to different phones as they change, keeping the same main number.

Questions to consider

Do you actually need a physical office?

How much time a week could you release by not commuting?

What working hours would suit your clients, and you, best?

How can people contact you when you are busy? Is your current method costing you sales?

Face to face networking

In my first book, Chocks Away, I talk about combining online and offline networking and how the skills are similar in both.

It's important to realise, as for online networking, you need to define what your goal is and pick events that are most likely to help you achieve that goal.

I've been attending networking events regularly since 2006, and have met many thousands of people in that time.

You meet a huge variety of people at events, *the purpose of which is to make connections that could lead to possible business rather than make a sale on the day.* That's an important point that is often missed.

In the years I have been networking I have attended events ranging from small ones with a handful of people right up to the larger ones with nearly 1,000 people.

At one event in London, the presenter asked the audience 'who is here to sell today?' and most of the hands went up. He then asked 'who is here to buy today?' and out of 500 people only a few hands went up.

It's something that's important to remember, particularly if you have a service - you need to establish your credibility first.

Dr Ivan Misner, who has over 25 years experience in networking, has developed the VCP(R) process:

Visibility & Credibility = Profitability.

This is a great way to think of potential business relationships:

Visibility – being at a networking event with other quality businesses for example.

Credibility - you need to establish your experience and qualifications, which can take time, and in the example above it's unlikely that people are ready to buy right now in the room. Once your credibility is established then they are likely to do business, and also refer their contacts too.

Profitability – or the sale, where business is done.

In my time networking I have witnessed a couple of incidences where people have been so focussed on selling to the room that they tried to jump the process and go from Visibility right to Profitability, with the result that they actually missed out on potential sales:

I was at an event in Guildford several years ago, there was a chap there who was approached by a bookkeeper – he just looked at her name badge, said 'I don't need bookkeeping' and walked off! What he didn't know was that the bookkeeper was approaching him because they needed HIS services. He could have actually made a sale if he hadn't been focussed on selling.

At another event there was a person who wanted to jump right to the sale. They had attended an event with quality business people in attendance but wanted to sell to the room that day, and became somewhat fractious when they couldn't. Rather than use it as an opportunity to get to know people, to start to develop relationships and establish their credibility, they wasted the chance.

It's important to remember that you don't know who the people in the room know – they could have the ideal contact or referral for you, but if you focus on selling to them then it's unlikely they will make the connection for you.

If you take the time to establish your credibility though, and are genuinely interested in other people at the event then the rewards can be very worthwhile.

Business cards

When people meet they usually exchange business cards, which can be a great opportunity to create a good first impression...or an opportunity to give a less than ideal impression, as there can be several points that people starting out (and even those in business for a while) don't realise.

Even in today's online world, a business card is a quick way to give people your contact details so that they can proceed further after the meeting. However, the card could actually be counting against you if you have any of these five issues:

Use your free email address. This is something that is maybe a few pounds a year to fix, but comes up regularly. Even if you don't have a website of our own you can pay for a personal email address, which will create a much better impression rather than using a free email account. I have seen people's business cards with a free account address many times, and I have even seen it repeated in foot high letters on the sides of their vans. With a personal email address people are likely to take you more seriously.

Only give a mobile phone number. How do people know that you didn't purchase a £10 burn phone, intending to throw it away after making some money? It's important to think about the impression this gives, particularly if that is the only means of contact.

Have inadequate contact details. Whilst you don't have to clutter the card with every possible way people can contact you mentioned, you do have to ensure that at least the main methods are covered such as phone, email and website if you have one. I have even had cards from people who didn't have any of these. They probably thought they were being clever, but a Google search of their name and business produced no results, so their card went straight into the recycling bin.

Use poor quality printing. Whilst you don't have to spend many hundreds of pounds on extremely expensive customised business cards, they do have to be reasonable. I've been at meetings where two people gave me a card with the same logo on it – I'd assumed they were from the same business but actually found out they'd just used a vending machine to print their business cards and chosen the same options! Reasonable business cards are affordable and a great way to stand out from others who think it doesn't matter.

Don't bring them. After going to the trouble of getting a good email address and phone number, then having reasonable quality cards produced, they are no good if you don't have them with you. I have been to many meetings where people did not have their business cards with them. At one meeting a lady even hand wrote a few on napkins! If you are travelling by car, keeping a box in the car means you always have them with you. If travelling otherwise a box always in your meeting bag or folder will ensure the same result. I discovered pocket card cases, that hold around 30 cards, and also always have one in whichever jacket I'm wearing to a meeting.

Business cards and the contact details on them are a great way to make a good first impression, and an easy way to stand out from your competitors.

After always using professional cards meeting these requirements myself I had an interesting experience at a meeting in the summer of 2012 when I had no choice but to break one of my own 5 rules for business cards.

I had one days notice before I was attending a networking meeting and required a card with my new domain. There was no way to get professional cards printed in time so my choice was either to bring no cards or to print them myself using a home card kit.

I chose to print them myself, and it was interesting to see the reactions from some of the meeting attendees - proving my point about printing above. One attendee even refused to take my card when offered, and handed it back to me!

Networking goals

There's a famous quote by Sir Alan Sugar , "business networking is a complete waste of time, all it is is people sitting around and just drinking some coffee."

Well it can be that case but it doesn't have to be...

It's important to know specifically why you're doing it and what you hope to achieve.

Perhaps it could be one of the three things below:

New business, are you looking to network so that you can actually bring in some more clients for your business?

Visibility, is it just something that you are doing to let people in the local area know about your business?

Socialising, running a business can be a lonely time for some people moving from employment, are you networking so that you can meet like-minded business owners?

Taking new business first, it's important to understand your strategy for this. As I mentioned, you probably won't actually get a lot of the new business on the day. What you do have though is the chance of developing relationships that can then lead to new business over time.

When we're looking at businesses it is important to understand the difference between leads and referrals. A lead is just someone who says 'I heard someone down the road is looking for an accountant.' there is no introduction or expectation of your call and it's very much just 'here is their phone number.'

Whereas a referral is someone who has actually gone out and looked for the business for you, recommended you and has actually made that connection.

That's one of the key differences to understand - if you're looking for new business, you might be better off with a referral organisation rather than a networking organisation.

If you're networking just for visibility it's important to understand your target market and who you are trying to reach. If you're dealing with small individual self-employed clients what you may find is that if you went to a large Chamber of Commerce, the connections you'd make there wouldn't actually generate too much business though.

You never know who someone knows, so there is always the possibility of business but perhaps your time would be better invested in an environment with a higher chance of success. It's important to find the type of event that's going to bring you that business and then to seek that out and to do more of them rather than just go to a lot of networking events and spread yourself too thinly.

Now if you're networking for socialising, that could be socialising just for its own ends. But what you can find is that you can actually get business from it, without even trying.

We've all heard of the people doing business on the golf course and you too could find that you get business just from socialising. But the important thing to remember is don't treat a social event exactly like a business event. You wouldn't run around the golf club handing out business cards trying to make connections, whereas that may be appropriate at a speed networking event. So remember if you are socialising, keep it mainly social.

With all different types of networking, remember to consider the connections *outside* the room...

If you go to a networking event and there's 30 people in the room you might think that if you make 30 sales to these people then there isn't any more business to be done.

But the statistics show the average person now has 1,000 connections. So it's not the 30 people in the room that you should be concentrating on, it's the 30,000 people they are connected to through their connections.

Another thing you may hear is the term hunting versus farming. Now with hunting I've seen that myself, people run into the room and try do business with people in the room straightaway. They are looking for a quick hit and then they can move on to the next event. I've even had a financial adviser ask me to refer all my clients to them, after only meeting them for the first time five minutes beforehand!

Farming is different, what we're actually looking at is developing relationships over time that would lead to business in the future. In the end it could bring you much more business than hunting, but it's going to take time to build up those relationships though.

So when you looking at networking don't be focussed on instantly getting business. Networking is not a get rich quick scheme but, in order to get rich *it's very much something that you are going to have to invest time in over a number of months.*

Questions to consider

What's the most unusual business card you have seen? How did it help you remember them?

What are your own goals for networking?

How much time are you willing to invest in networking?

Do you need to learn new networking skills? If so, how are you going to acquire them? (perhaps via training courses, online or via books?)

Social Media

My first book was published back in 2010.

Two years is a long time in Social Media, we have seen new sites rise and others fall – and the speed in which this happens has been increasing.

Whilst the sites people use may change, what remains constant are the techniques I use with Social Networking for business – after all it is just *being Social with a network*.

With so many different platforms available it can be difficult for people new to Social Media to decide where to start. My own recommendation is to use twitter, as it is limited to messages the size of a standard SMS text it is easy to pick up without taking too much time. I have included an updated version of my getting started with twitter guide in the appendix.

Being present

In the modern world with access to Social Media channels as well as mobile devices there is now the opportunity to be connected 24/7. In effect you can be in two places at once... but are you really fully present at either of them?

To quote the famous Goldblum line "just because you can, doesn't mean you should" – particularly when the end result could be a loss in credibility.

Dr Ivan Misner mentioned in his blog 'Don't Make This Mistake at Your Next Networking Event' about the dangers of trying to do two things at the same time and the effect on credibility. He talks about networking meetings specifically in his blog, but unfortunately whilst you would think people would understand that if you were in a normal meeting with a client you wouldn't take a call would be obvious, I occasionally come across people that don't quite get this.

Indeed I had someone a while ago who was upset I didn't take their call half way through another meeting! How would they have felt if I was meeting with them instead and I stopped to take a call? I've been in meetings where the other person has pulled out their ringing mobile phone and actually answered it! Not only is this disrespectful to the person they are with, it also disrespects the caller as they are not able to give them their full attention.

It's important to recognise boundaries, and whilst it might be ok to share something online during certain meetings if it is appropriate – it's not usually ok though when in a private meeting.

Being able to turn off the 24/7 communication is an increasingly important skill as the differing methods and the volume will only increase. When I am with a client, I am completely present and not reachable externally. In fact, I actually removed my mobile phone number from my business cards last year and don't give it out except where it is necessary for a specific meeting.

This doesn't mean that I am out of touch – I have an excellent PA who handles my calls, should there be an extreme emergency (rare in tax as the deadlines are all well known) she can contact me on my cell phone if it's appropriate.

Between meetings I can check on my messages and respond, but not during the meeting – for that time I am wholly present at the meeting.

Some people may think that juggling multiple cell phones, social media accounts and face to face meetings makes them super productive – but they could find that they are actually affecting their credibility, as well as not achieving their best productivity.

Using automation

It's important to be present where you are but there is a trick you can use to give *the appearance* of being somewhere else... this is the use of update scheduling, something that if used correctly can increase your effectiveness.

For example, while I was out enjoying a woodland walk one day my blog was updated with a post and our monthly client mailing was issued as well.

I had pre-prepared both of these and set them to be issued automatically – most software has the option of scheduling an update, whether it is a blog, mailing or a social media update.

Used sparingly, this can be a good way to maintain regular contact when you know you are going to be concentrating on something else. It's important to make sure they are used sparingly though – social networking isn't broadcast networking.

I've seen people make that mistake and use them to blast out sales messages 24/7. I have also seen the curious case where two auto responders that had been set up were having a 'conversation' between themselves on social media!

One other thing to be aware of though with automated postings is time – specifically night time. When your update goes out will affect your credibility. People who don't know about automation will wonder why you were up at that time of night and if you are someone they would want to do business with the next day.

In addition, sending out updates in the middle of the night means that your local audience is tiny compared to during the day, and the chances of your posting being missed are high. I have seen a professional who had their twitter account set up to blast out several messages an hour 24 hours a day – with a UK market it's unlikely anyone would be interested at 1am, and when people see the time of the posting it's going to form part of their opinion about the poster.

You also have to consider the possibility that too many sales messages will be seen as 'interruption marketing' that is distracting from people's focus, and in the modern world has less place than traditionally.

If you haven't heard of the term 'interruption marketing' before, one example could be:

Someone comes to your office without an appointment to sell you something you hadn't asked for.

You may listen to their pitch and decide it's not for you – so politely tell them so and go back to what you were working on.

10 minutes later they come back and give their pitch again…

It wouldn't be acceptable in the offline world, so it shouldn't be acceptable online either.

Many people now have a policy of automatically deleting unsolicited emails, without even looking at them, similarly for direct mail and 'over sharing' on social media.

There could still be a place for these as part of an overall marketing strategy, but it is important to understand that they need to be targeted and of interest if they are to be successful.

My view is that the online and offline worlds are very similar, so you shouldn't do something online that you wouldn't do in a face to face meeting.

Sharing slides

One other social media site you may want to check out is slideshare. You may not have heard about this site before, which lets you easily share presentation slides on the web – and let people download a copy should it be set to allow this.

I uploaded an updated version of my 'more time and money via social media' presentation to slideshare in August 2012, and it generated a lot of interest…

so much so that I had an email the next day from slideshare to tell me that my presentation was being talked about more on LinkedIn than anything else from slideshare! When you consider LinkedIn has over 150 million members, that is a significant achievement.

As a result, they also featured my presentation on the slideshare home page – and the views will continue to increase over time as more people discover it.

Security on social media

An area that may concern people using social media is personal security, particularly with location based services.

You may not have heard of these before, basically they are easy ways of sharing where you are and what you are doing. Usually accessed by an app on your phone that uses the built in GPS, benefits can include:

- easy ways to share pictures
- a map of your location
- possible special offers from locations you visit.

The update can also be pushed to twitter or Facebook as well as your app contacts...

But, who's listening?

One of the great things with Social Media is its openness, and the fact that your messages have the potential to be seen by millions...

however when it comes to personal security this might not always be the best thing as your updates could be public, and do you really know who all your online connections are?

What's the solution?

There are several methods you can adopt to increase your safety, some of them are below:

1) Check in when you check out – rather than saying where you are now you can say where you have been.

2) Delay your status updates – rather than telling people 'I'm going to be out of the office all day today at x, y z' you can post it the next day telling people where you have been.

3) Be vague in locations – rather than saying 'I'm on the 8:05 to waterloo again' or similar, be purposely non specific.

4) Security settings – there may be an option to hide your location check in, so you can still benefit from any special offers but aren't publicly broadcasting your location.

Online security very much applies to the information in your profile too, so you may want to edit the details of what you are sharing (full dates of birth, full addresses, etc aren't necessary on a public personal profile.)

I have been using Social Media both personally and in my business since 2008 and haven't had any issues, so you just need to be aware of the public information that you are sharing and ask yourself...

if I wasn't in front of a computer or smartphone, would I be telling everyone around me exactly what I'm doing and where I am?

Performance scoring

When using online networking you may come across sites that say that they will give you a score out of 100 for your 'online value.'

I have been noticing increasing frustration from people with sites such as these, where they are spending large amounts of time trying to get their score up and being frustrated when the result doesn't match the effort.

Some of the sites even claim to give you a share value. There's a difference between a business simulation that has genuine learning opportunity, and a game.

The dictionary definitions are:

- A simulation is an enactment, as of something anticipated or in testing.

- A game is an amusement or pastime.

It's important to remember these definitions when considering business activities. Simulations and games have their place but this needs to be considered in respect to actual goals and plans.

Taking my own experience as a pilot, I've used flight simulators during my flight training and they do have their place as they have been developed by experts over many years with many millions of pounds worth of investment.

Similarly I know of a business simulation developed from real world experience that is used in teams, with expert guidance, to help companies increase their results. With simulations they can be used as a tool in relation to real world activities, and the best results do come when combined with the guidance of an expert who has that actual experience, following a structured agenda.

Games do not require the same level of detail as simulations, so whilst they may be enjoyable their value in building relevant experience is limited.

Of course playing games can have a secondary networking function, just like the traditional networking that takes place on the golf course and the squash court/etc. but this is a secondary effect.

If you can demonstrate a positive ROI on the time spent playing games, then it's worthwhile – otherwise it's 'NOTworking' instead of networking.

Simulations can give you help in formulating plans (provided they are based on sufficient amounts of real world data) but don't confuse games with reality, at the end of the day making a million credits on a simple game isn't a million pounds in the real world.

Having signed up to these sites myself to get an insider's view, and been 'successful' there, I deleted my profiles and... nothing happened! The world didn't end as some people predict.

There was a comment I read a while ago from Chris Voss about one particular site, that applies to all of these public sites that claim to 'rank' you (according to their own rules) that I very much agree with:

"Companies spend millions of dollars to have people mentally ASSOCIATE their brands with success and positivity. Since most companies can't be online all the time, their stock eventually loses. On discussion boards Companies and Brands get kicked around and trashed with the association of their name as "losers." They are listed in categories as Losers. It doesn't seem that smart to me."

As I say in my first book, the combination of online and offline networking can bring great results – but be aware of activity that feels like work but isn't.

Your online profile

One thing in common, no matter what site you are using, is the public profile.

With the large numbers of sites available, a way to save time is to spend some in the beginning creating a profile that is transportable between them.

Profiles now can range from perhaps your hobbies through to maybe what could be considered an online CV – many sites have similar elements and you can customise your profile for each once you have a base one.

Another thing to remember is that your profile picture, or avatar, is the representation of you online – it is worth paying a professional photographer to take a headshot that you can use online. Keeping this profile picture is important as people will use it to recognise you online, so if you keep changing your picture every few days it is likely to reduce the interaction you get online as people won't recognise you.

Backups are another thing to consider, particularly with longer profiles you create. I've learnt this the hard way, there was a site I used to use that you had to program your profile in HTML code – one slip in entering or updating this and your profile was lost!

Again, if the site should not be available anymore you want to be able to have your profile stored for easy access and uploading to new sites.

Another point to consider is where your online profile is stored.

Every Social Networking site has a different audience so you may have various profiles on different sites. Each site will have their own rules as to what you can put in your profile, and the format of that entry – If we consider that online you are your profile, in effect you are renting the space on their site and you have to follow the rules of the rental.

This may be fine for you, depending on the site and the rules, however if you want to develop a deeper profile you may find yourself restricted. I would recommend, in addition to any profiles you have on successful sites, that you create your own profile space on the web - buying your own place instead of renting. The cost of a domain name is very affordable, and you can then create exactly the profile you want there under your own rules.

Indeed, that is the reason I created www.jamesmcbrearty.com so that I have one in-depth, fully customisable digital presence on the web in addition to the smaller cut down profiles on various sites.

Media Integration

The integration of the web & TV has been talked about for some time, it was interesting to see it in action a while ago.

The Dragons TV shows have people pitching their business idea to potential investors, and is a popular one that also has its own versions in many countries.

On one show there was a pitch for a website that dealt with present lists for children. Watching the show, I thought I would check out the site so grabbed my iPad to look it up – only to find that it didn't seem to be working. I had thought that this was a lost opportunity, until I found out that the reason it wasn't working is that it had over 1.4 million hits!

This shows just how many people were multitasking and using the web, probably on a mobile device, whilst watching TV.

In addition, I was also communicating with several people on twitter at the same time when watching and we were discussing the show. You no longer have to wait to discuss shows the next day, now you can do this while they are still being broadcast.

The increasing use of mobile web, via smartphones and tablets, is an important one – indeed I changed the video hosting on my taxhelp.uk.com website to YouTube a few years ago so that people using iPads and iPhones, and other devices without flash, could access my videos directly.

Online netWORKing

Finally in this chapter, I'd like to consider the hidden costs of online networking that you need to be aware of.

Dr Ivan Misner, the founder of BNI, has a perfect description for business networking:

"it's not net sit or net eat, it's net WORK."

I've been involved with using online networking in my business since 2008 and just as for offline networking this is something to be aware of online – particularly with the emergence of social gaming.

Seth Godin posted a blog in March 2011 'Are you making something?' which raises some important points:

More and more, we're finding it easy to get engaged with activities that feel like work, but aren't. I can appear just as engaged (and probably enjoy some of the same endorphins) when I beat someone in Words With Friends as I do when I'm writing the chapter for a new book. The challenge is that the pleasure from winning a game fades fast, but writing a book contributes to readers (and to me) for years to come. The boss (and even our honest selves) would probably freak out if we took hours of ping pong breaks while at the office, but spending the same amount of time engaged with others online is easier to rationalise.

It's important to have a goal of what you want to achieve online, for example whether it is increased visibility, customer support or new client acquisition.

Once you have the goal you can then come up with a plan to achieve it, such as allocating a specific time in the diary and setting out what you want to achieve in that time.

When you are networking online it is easy to be diverted if you don't have a goal and plan, with the result that you can actually be 'notworking' instead of networking.

I was disturbed to read a blog where someone had mentioned that they hadn't achieved much over the last few years online using a particular website, only to be told by several posters that they hadn't given it enough time and should continue – a real danger of confusing notworking and networking.

Thinking about this, I wondered what the impact on a business could be if they continued with unproductive notworking online:

Assuming someone is spending one hour a day (many people spend more than this) the costs per year would be:

1 hour x say 240 work days a year = 240 hours lost.

Assuming an average charge out rate for a business owner of £100/hour this means that the cost of notworking is: £24,000 a year !

When you look at what notworking online could be costing you, it's important to make sure that what you are doing is taking you closer towards the goals you have set.

Questions to consider

Are you fully present where you are?

Could automatic updates enable you to increase your productivity?

What are your online goals?

When spending time online, are you making something?

Video for business

I've been using video for business since 2009, and seen great results. The videos I initially created were of me being interviewed about taxhelp.uk.com, explaining the services and how we work with clients to make things as easy as possible.

These were then integrated into our website so that visitors had the option of watching the video or listening to the audio as well as reading the copy on the website.

Shortly after the videos went live I had a rather unusual meeting with a new client, someone I had never met before. The meeting took around 20 minutes, which was half the time of an average new client meeting beforehand.

The reason for this was the videos online – the client had in effect already 'met' me and covered the basics that I had in the past had to explain to people at every meeting.

So, whilst it took some time away from the office, and a financial investment, to create these videos the result was an increased conversion level and a saving in time from future meetings.

My videos are working 24/7 generating enquiries and answering questions – whenever it is convenient for the viewer to watch.

YouTube opportunities
You may be surprised to hear that you can actually get clients directly from YouTube.

I've had several myself, a point that people miss is that YouTube is actually also the world's second biggest search engine. The use of web video is still low in several areas, so it is a great way to stand out from your competitors - and as with all social media, the sooner you start the harder it is for competitors to catch up.

When a video is uploaded it is searchable by people, and they could be looking for your advice and product or services.

As I've found myself, referrals from web video have a higher conversion rate and the subsequent meetings are shorter so there is a double benefit.

You can even have your own TV channel now, thanks to YouTube.

A few years back this would have been almost impossible, the barriers to entry of costs and technical knowledge would have prevented it.

Now it is possible to have your own TV channel for free. It is very easy to register on the site and set up a page yourself.

I set up the taxhelp.uk.com YouTube TV channel back in March 2009 and have been updating it since then with new videos. You may worry about being able to create content, indeed my own content level was fairly low in the past but this has been increasing significantly in 2012.

Like blogging, you may find that creating video becomes easier the more that you do it.

If you have a modern mobile phone you might find that it is able to shoot high-definition video, so you already have the equipment you need. Once you have the video you may need to edit it before uploading, again this can be done very easily - even directly on the phone itself.

With different people responding to different communication methods, you could find that having a video increases the potential clients you are reaching as well as helping existing ones.

You don't even have to be on film yourself to create web videos, I have recorded several where they have been web walkthroughs of sites - recording the screen with an audio track on top.

Another option I have used is the animoto website, which creates videos from pictures and video clips you have uploaded. I used this site to create my entry for the 2012 BNI video competition.

Questions to consider

Perhaps business video is something you want to investigate yourself?

Would you like to have shorter, more productive meetings?

Do you already have the basic equipment to get started with video and trial it?

Would you like another salesperson, working 24/7 to promote your business - for free?

Blogging

There seems to be a lot of confusion regarding Social Media, and that it is a new technology.

What is Social Media? Well, if you go back to basics and examine the words – it's just being Social with a Media!

My own view is that it is in fact an old concept; all that has changed now is the method of delivery. As I say on the cover of my first book, "The means can easily complicate the ends."

Taking blogging as an example of how things haven't really suddenly changed, Wikipedia says a blog can be commentary or news on a particular subject. The ability to leave comments in an interactive format is an important part of many blogs.

BUT, we had that back in 1872!

In the UK we have 'speakers corner' a place where individuals can publicly share their thoughts in an interactive environment. It's the same in many other countries.

The potential audience for your 'blog' was smaller then, comprised of the people actually there in the audience as well as others who they shared your blog with but the principle was the same.

In the past there were large barriers to entry in the traditional media, whereas today an individual's blog can have the same influence as a major news organisation.

Indeed several blogs have actually been quoted and featured by the media.

One of the points I raise in my presentations is that there isn't that much difference in the online and offline worlds. I have had the experience of joining BNI and starting in Social Media at the same time back in 2008, so I have seen the similarities in my journey with them both.

Yes, there are some differences to be aware of, but it's important not to become hung up on the media you use

– it's being social that matters.

If you take things back further, Nick Tadd made a great point on a blog in 2009:

"I would argue that social media goes back to the time of cavemen. Instead of twitter they had red ochre, a finger and a cave wall, which they shared information – maybe about how to bring down mammoths?"

Increased website traffic

As with several aspects of social media, the misconception may be that it does not have a direct business return that can be easily measured.

When it comes to blogs though, there is data out there to prove the direct business results that can be achieved – and an increase in hits to a website is one easy way that can be measured in real-time. (In addition to all the other benefits that come as a result.)

I was at a branding master class meeting in Guildford when one of the attendees shared an amazing statistic from Sarah Orchard, who was a key speaker at The Big eCommerce Conference:

- a blog with 100 posts sees three times more traffic than one with 50 posts.

- by blogging twice a week you will receive three times more traffic than somebody blogging once a week.

These are amazing statistics, so I decided to perform my own test. For a period of two weeks I blogged every day, the result was...I increased my website traffic by nearly double... and had a record 10,000 hits one week.

Whilst blogging every day isn't something that many people can sustain, it does prove the point. As a result of that I do plan to blog once a week as a minimum, which is something that can easily be achieved.

For myself, I tend to get in the writing zone and produce batches of blogs together. Thanks to the scheduling features of my website these can be set to issue one per week – no matter where I happen to be that day.

Have you tried business blogging yet? It could be a great way to increase traffic and engagement, and the only cost is your own time.

How often should you post a blog?
One point that can put people off, before they even start – how often should I post a blog?

The more often you are posting, the more traffic you should receive to your site. When you are starting out you may only post one blog a month, which is fine if you post one *every month*.

When I am looking at other people's blogs, if the last post was six months ago then it gives the appearance that they may have stopped. Regular posting will give you a greater impression and let readers know that your site is current.

There are also search engine benefits to regular updating, as if a site is being regularly updated then it will be seen to be active, rather than one that has a reducing interest and relevancy, so will rank higher.

If you are interested in the amount of traffic coming to your site then your goal should be to aim to post one blog a week, which with some experience is fairly straightforward to do with practice. If you can do more than this, then the benefits will increase.

How long should a blog post be?

People can be put off blogging by the thought of having to write a set number of words. If you are writing a post for someone else they may have a requirement of say 500 or 1000 words, which can be a struggle for those starting out.

The good news is that blog posts appear to be getting shorter, readers want advice that is to the point rather than a long rambling post that has been padded out to reach a set number of words.

If you are posting on your own blog, feel free to write posts that are of whichever length you like – frequency is an important factor so if shorter postings help you to achieve this then they are to be welcomed.

Your posts should always have value though - just posting something because you think you should is likely to cost you readers.

What is your blog called?
I learned a while ago that being called blog isn't good enough.

I've been blogging since 2009, my first blog was simply called 'James McBrearty's blog.' I took a day out of the office to attend a blogging course so I could take my blogging to higher levels. One of the results was the new name for my blog – 'achieving freedom', you may ask what's the significance of the name and there are several:

I help people achieve freedom from the 9 to 5 by starting their own business and the tips I share in the blog reflect that. It's also something I've done myself leaving the corporate world.

I also help people achieve freedom from paying too much tax, and this is also something I cover in the blog.

Networking and public speaking always rate higher than death in surveys of people's greatest fears! Having started doing these on my own without any support, this is something I can identify with and help people achieve freedom from those fears.

In my spare time I fly aeroplanes (I've held both European and American private pilots licences for over 10 years) so

I achieve freedom from gravity! There are also tips I can share from the flying world that very much apply to the business world.

The name of your blog defines it, and once you have this it can assist with creating content, as you have a focus for your postings.

Inflammatory blogs

I learned about someone who deliberately posts controversial blogs. Used sparingly, this can be an effective way to stimulate debate and also raise your visibility.

However...... if it is used too often it can have a negative effect on your credibility.

An example of a similar situation is a certain airline here in the UK – making preposterous press releases about future plans just to incense people and kick off debates.

Yes, it did work a few times initially and generated a fair amount of press coverage, however it has been overused and in my own opinion has now damaged their credibility with me. I just now ignore whatever press release they issue, as I'm sure others do too.

If you are blogging just to incense people you need to be aware of the effect on your credibility if you do it too often.

Questions to consider

Can you see the potential business benefits to blogging?

What could you blogs be called & what does would it stand for?

How often do you intend to blog?

How will you ensure that you keep creating content, and not stop after a few updates? (perhaps planning out 12 months blog titles now could help?)

Video Blogging (vlogging)

I have seen the benefits of blogging as well as the benefits of using video, so it seemed obvious to combine the two.

Video blogging is fairly new to me, having only started in mid 2012, but I have already seen the possibilities of the combination through increased visibility.

It still involves writing a script of what you want to cover, as for a standard blog, but this is recorded on video instead of by text.

When recording video blogs the best duration seems to be 2 to 3 minutes long. Even though you may have great points to make, if people see a video length longer than this they are unlikely to even start to watch it.

With a video blog on YouTube you can also upload a text transcript, so you are fully covered - the audience then have the opportunity to watch the video, listen to the audio or read the text.

Vlogging is a great way to get ahead of your competitors, as there are quite a few people who have not adopted it yet.

Rather than just use the webcam built into a laptop screen, there are good possibilities for location variation with vlogging. I have shot vlogs in my own studio, in offices performing interviews, as well as in the countryside.

There are no limits to what you can film and as long as the video is something people want to watch then you can find it brings in more visibility than just text alone.

With blogging and vlogging they can be combined - there are different audience members on my YouTube channel compared to my blog, so cross posting when appropriate is a good opportunity. I may record a vlog, then embed it into a later blog so that this can be seen there as well.

Embedding is an additional benefit as well, if you upload a video to YouTube it is then easy to share. You can use it as a response to someone else's blog, or use it on a page of your website to illustrate a point.

There are some differences between vlogs and professional videos, so I use both in combination.

Below I share some of the points I have learned about vlogging, that make a big difference to the end result. Although the message of the vlog is important, when using the medium of video it has to appeal.

Video quality

Viewers could be watching your vlog on a 50" TV, thanks to many devices that let you access YouTube on TV. It's therefore important to consider the quality of your video.

The device you use will play an important part in this, while most cameras and phones have been able to record video for some time they may not be up to the task for regular use.

If you are shooting a vlog yourself you will most likely be using the camera with the lens pointing towards you. You therefore need a forward facing screen to see what is being recorded to ensure you are in frame.

Whilst some mobile phones allow you to do this, the front facing camera is usually much lower quality than the main camera. If you want to shoot something quickly then it may be ok for the occasional vlog, but in the long term you will want something better.

The best solution may well be a camcorder. They are very affordable now and some are even pocket sized so they are easy to carry with you.

If you go for one that is 720P HD or above, then the quality will be fine when viewed on a large screen.

For the best quality video using a tripod does make quite a difference. I have a pocket tripod that can be used when out of the studio and is ideal for situations such as interviews.

In order for the camera to record good quality video, it will need good lighting.

In the studio this can be easy to achieve as you are in a fixed location and can move lights around until you achieve the best combination.

Natural light works well, but restricts your filming to certain times of the day as I found out when I shot my first vlogs. I'd risen early to shoot several, but found that this wasn't possible at that time of day due to bright sunlight in my face at the location I'd chosen.

For studio lighting, modern camcorders work very well at adjusting the colour balance for artificial light, so you just need to arrange the lights.

I was recommended to use what is called '3 point lighting' by several people, this is a technique that forms the basis of many studio set ups and gives good contrast rather than being washed out by a bright light straight on:

- the main or key light is behind the camera, off to one side.

- there is a lower powered fill light on the other side to reduce shadows.

- behind the presenter there is a light as well, to highlight them.

The best way to illustrate this is if you go to YouTube and search for '3 point lighting' as the are some good videos illustrating the set up and including video of the results as they are combined.

When you are shooting video you will also want to think about your background. A plain wall is fine for most vlogs as it avoids distractions, perhaps a pop up banner can be used to give the impression of a red carpet interview.

I have seen quite a few accountant videos use the office/filing cabinet as a background - there are some people that say to do this as it shows your professional environment so it could be an option. But, I have seen messy filing cabinets stuffed with papers that distract from the message.

One good background I have seen is recording in front of a tidy bookcase, and if you have won awards then this can be a great opportunity to showcase them as well.

As well as the majority of studio vlogs, I also shoot various ones outside as this gives a different impression.

My professional videos for my websites were shot outside and it does generate more interest than an office background, as well as ensuring a calm atmosphere when people may be upset and looking for advice.

Audio

You may think that the camcorder records audio, and in a studio environment this may be sufficient however an external audio recorder may improve things and increase the quality, particularly when outdoors.

Sometimes the camcorder may have a socket to plug-in an external microphone, otherwise you can use a voice recorder connected to an external microphone and combine the video and audio at the edit stage.

You don't need one of those large fluffy microphones on a boom, a simple lapel mic will suffice - and as they are designed to capture voice they work well.

The audio quality is an important part of the video, indeed someone told me it could be 80% of the total impression. Some of my first vlogs were recorded on a HD bridge camera, but unfortunately the audio just wasn't good enough so it meant a change was needed for later videos.

Editing

Once you have the video and audio recorded it is unlikely that it will be in a format completely ready for broadcast, so will require editing.

I have shot vlogs in one take and this makes things easy as I just need to add my introduction, titles and ending to have a video ready for uploading.

Sometimes I take different sections I have recorded and combine them, or perhaps take one long vlog and separate it into smaller vlogs.

Editing is incredibly easy now, my earlier vlogs were edited on the iPad and I was able to pick up the basics very quickly.

Should you wish you can use software that allows you much greater control, although as with presentations you probably don't want to go overboard on the special effects.

Questions to consider

Could vlogging be suitable for your business?

Do you already have equipment that could be suitable?

Where will you shoot your videos & how often?

Can you shoot videos to demonstrate something, resulting in fewer enquiries for the same information and freeing up your time?

Using your financial accounts

There are some people who have their figures prepared once a year, then after filing the tax return just put them in a drawer.

Your financial accounts have a much greater value than just for reporting and paying tax, as they can be used to assist in planning decisions as well as reviewing the success of previous undertakings that you may have trialled.

As a result you will probably want to keep your records up to date each month for planning, and so that at the year-end you are ready to prepare the final accounts as soon as possible as well as knowing where you are from month to month.

If you leave things until the last minute, you could be trying to plan with information that is out of date and possibly miss out on opportunities to save tax or minimise outgoings.

One of my future books is a guide to understanding business accounts and using them for planning purposes - specifically targeted at the small business and in plain language. It will help business owners understand the things that can help them grow the business, rather than tell them how to prepare accounts.

You started your business to do the business, rather than become an accountant or bookkeeper - so getting help may be a worthwhile investment.

Hidden costs of completing your own tax return?

I occasionally meet people who may think that completing their own tax return saves them money, unfortunately when they add up all the hidden costs that they don't realise it can actually prove to be very expensive:

Your time - one that is most often overlooked. Completing your own tax return isn't free, it is costing you billable time that could be better spent earning money rather than trying to work out how to complete the tax return and accounts) When you consider that it may take several days to complete in total, that is a significant cost.

No tax relief on your time – your own time does not qualify for tax relief, so however long it takes you this can't be claimed for. Contrast this with accountancy fees that, for the self-employed, qualify for tax relief.

Missed deadlines – I have seen people who came to me for help where the penalties they have been charged for missing deadlines were more than our fees would have been. With an adviser you don't need to worry, as they remind you of upcoming deadlines so you can relax. When you consider that the fines for a late return can now amount to over £1600, even when there is no tax due, these can be significant.

Errors - I have seen people who ended up with tax bills of over £60,000 because they didn't understand the tax laws and claimed for expenses that were not allowable over a number of years.

Penalties – in cases where tax has not been correctly calculated and paid, this could leave people open to additional fines from HMRC – these can in some cases double the tax bill.

Changes - tax laws are constantly changing, indeed professionals such as myself are required by our professional bodies to complete many hours of continuing education each year to stay up to date with the changes. Not doing this could leave taxpayers open to fines and penalties as above.

Worry – with a professional adviser, you know that your affairs are dealt with for you, and you can relax.

When you add up these benefits, you may have a different view on 'saving money' by completing your own tax return. One of the things that people worry about before they see an adviser is what it is going to cost, you might think this is a simple question, based on how much they charge for the meeting... You will be pleased to find that the majority of accountants don't actually charge for an initial meeting, however there is an additional cost that you may not have counted – your time.

Most accountants work normal business hours, 9am – 5pm, which means you need to arrange to visit their office within those times. As well as the time for the meeting itself there is your commuting time to include, perhaps adding an hour or two & making it two to three hours in total.

Depending on what hourly rate you charge clients, that free meeting could easily cost you several hundred pounds in lost business. So, if you can find an accountant that also offers meetings in the evenings, early mornings and weekends it will save you money straightaway.

As well as the times of the meetings, it will help if you can meet an accountant at a location that's convenient to you – whether that is your home, your office or another convenient location for you.

When you look at the significant fines that HMRC are now charging for late returns, combined with the tax relief available on accountant's fees – getting help could actually cost you less than doing nothing, and you can also avoid all the worry as well.

What is an accountant?
When you hear the term accountant you may already have an image and think that you know what this is... however things are not always as they seem, and there can in fact be large differences between them.

Name
You may be surprised to find that the generic term 'accountant' isn't protected, and anyone can actually call themselves one – even if they have no experience or qualifications. (The term 'chartered accountant' is protected, but many people would not notice the distinction.)

Experience
Sometimes accountants start a business by buying a block of clients from a retiring accountant – this can be a quick way to get started as they have a ready business, however could mean that they miss out on the experience of starting a business from scratch which could be of use to you.

Specialism

A normal accountant could perhaps be considered to be likened to a GP – dealing with many aspects of accounts and tax, perhaps including payroll, limited companies and other areas. If you can find a specialist, their knowledge and experience will be more focussed.

Price

There are a few points you may want to consider in relation to the topic:

Is the price a quote or an estimate? Estimates can sometimes unfortunately be too low, resulting in a nasty surprise later.

Is VAT included? Many accountants quote fees excluding VAT, so you could find an extra 20% on top of the bill you had budgeted for if you are not VAT registered yourself.

Are there any extras? Do you have to add a cost for software to produce your data in a format they would like or are they flexible? ...and remember to include your own time cost for learning how to use their system and using it.

Are the prices open? Do you know up front what the packages are and their costs? Is this published, or do you need to find out at a meeting?

These are some of the issues that can affect you as the owner of a small business. With the web it is easy to do research on an accountant now online to answer these questions. You can then choose one that will meet your needs.

Keeping business records

Whether you choose to do your own bookkeeping or get help, you will still have to keep the invoices and receipts for the business.

Many people may know that they have to keep their self-employed business records for a number of years, in case HMRC ask to see them. The actual rules are for five years after the filing deadline – the current tax return for the year to 5th April 2012 must be filed by 31st January 2013, so records must be kept until 31 January 2018.

This can result in large amounts of paperwork needing to be stored, but one thing that people may have missed is that business records can now be stored electronically provided several requirements are met:

- All the information must be captured (both the front and back of invoices and receipts.)

- The information must be saved in a readable format (if you are scanning, many scanners save to PDF files.)

- You must keep a back-up. There are even services now that will scan your receipts, themselves or via an app/email and output the data in a file that can be imported into accounting systems.

As long as the requirements above are met then you could find that saving space also saves you time, plus you have the benefit that electronic files can be searched much more easily if you are looking for an elusive receipt.

Questions to consider

Are your business records up to date, so they can be used for planning?

How much is it actually costing you to do your own tax and accounts?

Does your current adviser, if you have one, meet your requirements?

Are you making use of technology to reduce your record keeping burden?

Presentations & seminars

For many people, giving presentations isn't something that they do regularly or enjoy. When people are surveyed, public speaking usually ranks higher in their fears than death!

Indeed, without training it can be a daunting task to give one – my first presentation to a local networking group lasted a whole ten seconds, when I had a minute slot to fill! Yet, I have given many presentations now to audiences of over 100 people and for several hours duration.

It's a skill I've learned, and it is very much one that others can also learn too. My own skills were honed in the supportive environment of the world's number one referral marketing organisation, BNI, so I thought it may be useful to revisit my journey to show how any journey can be made easier when broken down into small steps.

With this supportive environment, and with the training courses provided, I was slowly able to develop my skills and become more comfortable doing the sixty seconds presentation initially.

Soon it was time for my ten minute presentation and that went ok. Afterwards I was surprised how quickly the time seemed to go. After four months, I was offered the role of Secretary Treasurer. I took the role with both hands as it meant being part of the leadership team and having to make a short presentation at the front of the room to the chapter and visitors weekly, again with training and support.

Three months later I was asked if I would like to be Chapter Director. I really wasn't sure about this as I would be running the meetings each week and it would be quite a bit outside my comfort zone, however it was a supportive environment and I would receive further training in how to do it, so I accepted. Now I would be running the ninety minute meetings each week, when a few months before I could barely manage ten seconds! This went well and over my leadership term I was able to develop until I was fairly comfortable about presenting to a group of people.

Since my term as Chapter Director, I have presented to several different networking groups about my own business and also about social networking of which I am an advocate. Following on from that, I was offered my first large audience – a chance to present to fifty financial advisers in London and, armed with my BNI presenting experience, I accepted.

After my term as chapter director finished, I was then offered the chance to become a Director Consultant for BNI. This involves looking after chapters, presenting to them and running training courses for members. I had gone from someone who could barely speak 10 seconds initially to now training members in networking skills, and supporting them!

Thanks to my role as a Director Consultant I have travelled throughout Surrey, Kent and Essex giving presentations – both to local BNI groups as well as at special seminars we have run too. The audiences for these have been over 100 people in many cases.

In addition I have also presented internationally, running several trainings to BNI groups in Spain on topics ranging from referral skills to social media. When I look back to

2008 when I gave my first 10 second presentation, it has been the combination of training and a supportive environment that has helped me to develop to where I am today. It is a great privilege to help others along the same journey as myself in developing their presentation skills.

Perhaps joining a local networking group, or organisation that gives you the opportunity to speak in public, could help you too? Starting slowly, you could find your skills increasing each time you present and also find it gets easier too.

Questions to consider

Are there presenting opportunities available to you if you ask?

Could presenting raise your own visibility and perhaps result in new business?

What other benefits do you foresee by being able to give a presentation to a large audience?

Books

This is my second book, writing both of them has been a great experience as it enables you to take the time to record your achievements and see how they have been possible when initially it wouldn't have seemed so.   ,

There are also other benefits, from a business point of view you have easily shared content that can help others as well as establishing your credibility.

However, there are some that say you **must** have a book, which is something I don't tend to agree with myself. I was at a business meeting last year when, instead of passing round business cards, people started swapping books!

Yes, books can be great but only if the time is right for you. Rather than spend months on a book, I would suggest that concentrating on the revenue generating business first is perhaps likely to bring a greater result.

Should the time be right for you to write a book, then this chapter covers some tips to help - publishing a book is easy today, without the traditional issues that used to exist.

As for writing the book itself, you can do this in your spare time here and there - I tend to do most of my writing on the iPad, so it's easy to do whenever convenient, rather than having to sit down in front of a computer.

Each author will develop their own methods and preferences, an important point to consider is that if you use social media or blogs then *you are already an author - just in a different format.*

Self published or traditional publishing?

Many people ask how I published my first book, so I thought it would be useful to share my experiences here. The route I used was self publishing – which now has many advantages over traditional publishing.

Some people still think of self publishing as when you used to order a few thousand copies from a printer and they usually ended up in your garage while you tried to sell them yourself, over many years.

Things have really moved on, one of the great advantages with self publishing is speed – once you have a completed and edited manuscript it can become the printed book in your hand in under a week, and also available for people to buy online and in book shops within two weeks!

The traditional publishing world has long lead times, with many stores planning their promotions months in advance. There is no physical difference between my book and a traditionally published one – they are both of the same quality and have ISBN numbers so that they can be ordered through any book shop. One of the other advantages with self publishing is the development of 'print on demand' – if someone orders my book it may not actually physically exist at that time.

When the order is received the book is individually printed and bound, then delivered. This means that the garage full of books can be avoided, and the self publishing house I use deal with all the orders for me. The book is also available in the US and the UK as well as Europe – it is printed at a location nearest to where the order is placed and delivered from there, avoiding the time and expense of delivery from one location.

Book revisions also become easy - if I update the manuscript online then future orders for the book will be of the new version, rather than having many copies of the old version to either sell or recycle first.

Where the difference does arise at the moment is in the promotion of the book – traditional publishers have staff and experience in this, whereas with the self publishing route it is the author who needs to do this themselves.

For my first book, I have been featured in several magazines so far, and have been interviewed on the radio as well. I also have a website set up for the book, and have been featured on BNI.com and SuccessNet. There are opportunities for promotion, you just need to seek these out and put in the time. It does mean some multitasking as both a book promoter and author though.

Questions to consider

Could a book help with establishing your credibility?

Is it the right time now, or would later be preferable?

What format would suit you best - eBook or print, or both?

How do you plan to promote your book after publication?

Setbacks - temporary (& other)

Entrepreneurs are always looking at new opportunities, and pursuing those that they believe will succeed. Occasionally those opportunities may not work out as planned, however it is important to take time to recognise the successes along the way.

I discovered this quote online:

'no matter that it doesn't work out, you are still further ahead than anyone else who hasn't even tried.'

It's an important point to remember.

Using a personal example, I started a local networking group in 2012. It didn't work out as planned unfortunately.

I'd made the promise to the founder members and our visitors that I wouldn't let it become a breakfast club... as a result I made the difficult decision to close the group, however I had many successes over a period of four months that otherwise wouldn't have happened:

- Personally inviting 1500 local businesses to visit our group, also raising the profile of taxhelp.uk.com in the community.

- Welcoming over 100 visitors to our group over the same period, further increasing our exposure.

- Seeing actual business being passed between the members and visitors.

- Connecting local businesses so that future opportunities can be investigated in one to one meetings.

- Achieving a personal goal, a few years ago I wouldn't have thought that I could start and run a weekly networking meeting from scratch.

- Further developing my knowledge of local businesses in the area, particularly in relation to how they are advertising their businesses and their results from different methods.

You can also expect other setbacks, but these are just normal business ones such as the occasional client that doesn't turn up for a meeting, work performed that goes unpaid, and the occasional bad debt.

The thing to remember if any of these happen is that they are normal, while they may affect you it's important to get back working towards the next sale.

"Know when to fold 'em"

This is a decision not to be taken lightly, remember many people give up just before they reach success...

Occasionally a project may not work out, whilst problems are to be expected if there is a permanent shift in the market it might be time to reconsider things.

It can be difficult for entrepreneurs to walk away from something that they have invested time and money into, however it's important to know when that time has come.

As I did myself with the networking group, you do have to review all the facts regularly and take counsel before making a decision.

That's why it's important to set specific goals and timescales, there may be some setbacks as a normal part of business. But if your own personal deadline has been reached and you are nowhere near the goals you had set, then it's time to consider whether continuing is the right thing to do.

It's a very difficult decision, indeed many people do give up just before they succeed - but you do need to be realistic.

You could also find, as I did, that the experiences along the way lead to other projects.

Questions to consider

What have you done that didn't work out exactly to plan, but as a result you actually achieved more than if you hadn't started?

What can you learn from the experience that you can take forward?

Are there any projects you are involved in that are far from your planned goals? Is it time to reconsider them?

Final thought

"Don't listen to anyone who tells you that you can't do this or that. That's nonsense. Make up your mind ... then have a go at everything... never, never let them persuade you that things are too difficult or impossible." Douglas Bader

When I started taxhelp.uk.com in 2006, I had always been an employee working for other people. There are usually people telling you that being an employee is safer and that self employment is risky, but with the changes in the world economy is this still the case?

When we are seeing redundancies of tens of thousands of people, my own view is that being an employee is actually risky now and self employment has the potential to offer more security as well as flexibility.

There are many people who would like to start their own business but don't ever take that first step – indeed it took me several months of deliberating before I made that step myself.

If you are currently building your own business, remember the best tool to help you is to always keep learning - with the right knowledge and application you too can experience a power climb with your own success.

About the author

James McBrearty is the CEO of taxhelp.uk.com, a company specialising in helping self employed people pay less tax and avoid fines.

James has been involved in the financial side of business for over a quarter of a century, and has run his own business since 2006.

He started his own business from scratch, after leaving corporate life, so knows exactly what it is like to run and grow a small business having done it himself.

In addition, he has assisted many hundreds of small business owners, so knows of the typical issues that arise in small business.

He started using face to face and online networking for business in 2008 and has had great results. He now shares his experience by assisting other business owners to maximise the possibilities.

In 2010 his first book was published, a guide to combining online and offline networking to grow a business.

He also gives regular presentations.

James is dual qualified in tax and accounts, and holds a fellowship of his tax association. He also serves on the association's membership committee.

In his spare time, James is interested in aviation. He has held a private pilot's licence since 2000, and built up over 350 hours in his logbook since then.

Resources

You can find and join with James online at:

Twitter: @taxhelpukcom

Company: taxhelp.uk.com

Consultancy: opbusiness.co.uk

LinkedIn: uk.linkedin.com/in/taxhelpukcom

Facebook: facebook.com/taxhelpukcom

Blog: taxhelp.uk.com/blog

YouTube: youtube.com/taxhelpukcom

James recommends these books:

Networking like a Pro by Dr Ivan Misner
Published by Entrepreneur Press on 1 Jan 2010

The E Myth revisited by Michael Gerber
Published by HarperCollins, 3rd edition, on 8 Nov 1994

Appendix

Twitter - Social Media basics

What is twitter?
It is a simple way of connecting with people easily, both existing friends and new contacts, by the sharing of short one hundred and forty character messages.

One advantage of twitter is that you are limited to the size of a standard text message, which means that it is quick to use as you do not have to spend large amounts of time composing content.

Another key advantage of twitter is that you can include links to other web locations and articles within the message, rather than try to condense what you are saying into a short message.

Quite often I will see a blog or article on the web that is of interest to people and I will send out a short message saying why I like it and providing the link so that people can access it directly.

With the one hundred and forty character limit there are many services online that can shorten links into a few characters so that you are not using up the whole message with the web address.

Why bother?
Dell Computer has made over three *million* dollars directly attributable to Twitter.

It is a quick and easy way to make connections with people and also to share information.

Many websites now have a share button, such as at the bottom of my homepage taxhelp.uk.com – by including these on your website people are able to share your site very easily with a couple of mouse clicks, rather than having to copy the web address and then paste it into an email for example.

By creating content online, that has *value* to people following you, you are creating greater interest in what you do and from that you will find that as a result people will want to find out more and the hits on your website will increase over time.

You do have to ensure that you are providing information that is of interest and not just a different version of spam, where you constantly just try to get people to look at your site and don't engage in conversations.

Terminology
You will hear various terms mentioned to do with Twitter; the main ones are below and fairly simple to understand.

• 'Tweet' – this is like talking in open networking, it goes to all your friends *and the web*

• 'ReTweet' (RT) – telling your friends *(and the web)* something you heard from someone else

• 'Direct Message' (DM) – talking to someone in private

• #Hashtag - a way of defining a searchable and indexable term that relates to you, your expertise, your interest or products or services

Note that tweets and retweets are shared with the web and that they can be found by anyone who happens to be using a search term that is contained within your message. This is also a powerful way to use twitter as you can search for key words that are of interest to you and then connect with people using them.

If you keep your tweets to less than 100 characters, they can be easily retweeted by at least two other people. The retweet is powerful for two reasons. Firstly, your tweet is rebroadcast to other peoples' followers. Secondly, as someone else is recommending you, it can come with more gravitas and authority.

Also as Twitter search is real time you will get answers most closely related to what you are looking for. Whereas a web search may bring up articles and comments from months or years ago, a twitter search will bring up what people are talking about *now* which may only be minutes old.

First Steps
Here are the simple steps to get started with an account on twitter:

1) Go to twitter.com and register for an account

2) Search for people that you know and connect with them

3) See who they follow and if they are relevant then follow them too

4) Set up access on your mobile device – iPhones and Blackberries are particularly easy with good apps available for download

5) Download Tweetdeck for free on your computer, or an equivalent desktop program – it makes managing your account much easier. I also recommend Hootsuite.

6) Regularly update – at least once a day. I tend to update at least 5-10 times a day.

The last point is very important, so many people say 'I'm on Twitter' or 'I have a Twitter account' but unless you are updating at least once a day on average you really don't actually have an effective account. When potential followers look at your twitter page they will look at the last time you updated to see if you are someone worth following. If you haven't updated for several months then they are unlikely to want to follow you.

How to use twitter effectively

"Visibility > Credibility > Profitability"

You have to generate content for people first to have a chance for them to find you, which is your visibility. Creating content regularly will mean there is a greater chance of people reaching this stage.

From then the process is whether they will be interested in what you are saying, your credibility. If you just keep repeating the same message as a type of spam then this is unlikely. However if you are generating useful content and linking to useful information then they may do.

The final stage is whether they will be willing to do business with you, your profitability. This is the last stage of the process and *can't be rushed* – you have to go through the other stages before you reach the stage of actually doing business.

As to what I tweet about, when I started I may have been using twenty five percent business, twenty five percent social and half making connections by conversing with people. Again, it is not always just about business – people do business with *people,* and it is after all *social* networking.

An example of this is one of the new clients that came through Twitter – not because of something tax related that I tweeted about; this was simply because a conversation had been started when I asked for film recommendations.

I don't have a rigid set of rules that says I only tweet in these proportions – it is me posting the messages on the account so I will respond as I see fit. It is very much up to the individual as to how they use twitter, this is a guideline but there are no set rules apart from spamming.

Spamming, or 'chumming' as I heard Nick Tadd describe it is where people send you repeated impersonal sales messages. The great thing with twitter is that it is easily dealt with, offenders can be blocked and you won't be contacted by them again.

Recommended twitter users to follow:

Myself, for tips	@taxhelpukcom
Ivan Misner	@ivanmisner
Seth Godin	@sethgodin

Chocks Away

James's first book, published in 2010 and endorsed by Dr Ivan Misner, New York Times bestselling author & founder of BNI & Referral Institute:

"James McBrearty, through sharing his own experiences and knowledge, provides an invaluable guide to business owners worldwide. Businesses, like aircraft, can experience times of turbulence; Chocks Away: Achieving Freedom from the 9 to 5 will show you how to help your business takeoff, expertly navigate through economic fluctuations and changes in the global business climate, and land safely at the destination you planned for-instead of ending up somewhere else!"

There are many books on how to use online and offline networking in business ... but none quite like this.

With any new trend, it is easy to get swallowed up and consumed by the hype and miss the point completely.

The means can easily complicate the ends.

What James does in this book is bring a very healthy reality check into the equation ... namely why you should do this in the first place.

This book tells of James' personal journey to achieving freedom from the daily grind. It is full of tips for both newbie's and experienced networkers.

If you want to take control of your life and to allow your business to really take off, this is the book for you.

taxhelp.uk.com

taxhelp.uk.com is James McBrearty's company and it specialises in helping self employed people pay less tax and avoid fines.

It offers unique affordable packages, specifically designed to help the self employed sole trader make an easy decision to get help with their tax, rather than struggle on their own.

Many people think they are saving money by doing their own tax, but forget to account for the value of their own time and may also not be claiming for everything that they are entitled to, and could be overpaying tax.

At the time of writing the fixed fee packages are:

Bronze service – which provides the accounts and the personal tax return, and is completed from summary details provided by the client, such as a spreadsheet.

Silver service – as for the bronze service, this also includes bookkeeping so instead of the summary spreadsheet the client simply hands over the paperwork for processing.

Gold service – this is for special cases with more complex tax affairs, such as people with several businesses or multiple rental properties.

Of course the fees for these services are also an allowable business expense and qualify for tax relief in the accounts, making them even more affordable. Receiving tax relief for advice helping you to pay less tax is always of great interest to clients.

The service makes it easy for people to get help with their tax and take away the worry as appointments can be made at a time and place to suit the client – rather than them have to take time away from their business to travel to the office. There are also several appointments available in the evenings and at the weekends to make it even easier.

People are often concerned about asking questions in case they receive a bill for the time - by offering fixed fees that include queries on the return as part of the package, clients can be reassured about this and any questions can be answered quickly to put their mind at rest.

The reason taxhelp.uk.com are able to keep the fees so reasonable is because of the high levels of referrals they receive from clients; the happier the clients are, the more likely those clients are to recommend taxhelp.uk.com's services.

http://taxhelp.uk.com

OP Business

Is James's consultancy, specialising in One Person Businesses – helping them to earn more and spend less time in their business, so they can relax and do the things that they enjoy rather than the things they'd never intended to do.

Running your own business can be hard, without guidance you may waste time trying things that don't work out or you may be missing things that could increase your income and reduce the time you have to spend working.

Business mentoring specifically for the self-employed person, with no mumbo jumbo, long contracts or scary fees.

Sometimes you can be too close to the business to see things that should be apparent – a mentor can help with this.

Guidance and feedback from someone who has started a business from scratch and has grown it over six years, with significant increases in turnover and profit every year – and whilst in a recession.

James McBrearty has been involved in finance and accountancy for over a quarter of a century, and brings experience helping thousands of self-employed people. He has also run training seminars internationally.

http://www.opbusiness.co.uk

www.ingramcontent.com/pod-product-compliance
Lightning Source LLC
Chambersburg PA
CBHW052016230326

41598CB00078B/3494